My Torn
Dance Card

Also by David James

A Heart Out of This World
She Dances Like Mussolini

My Torn Dance Card

poems

David James

The Fly Came Near It
Flint, Michigan

The Fly Came Near It, LLC
Flint, Michigan

Copyright © 2015 David L. James

All rights reserved. No part of this book may be reproduced in any form or by any means without the prior written permission of the author or the publisher, excepting brief quotes used in connection with reviews.

Cover and book design by K.M. Zahrt

Acknowledgements

Earlier versions of these poems appeared in the following:

Caliban: "Something Cryptic"
California Quarterly: "Getting There"
The Child of My Child: "Borrowed Shoes"
Collagist: "The Death in Your Face Game" and "A Shedding of Skin"
Driftwood Review: "The One After This"
Hieroglyph: "God Lost in the Bread Section"
Iconoclast: "On Your Terms"
Karamu: "The Pleasure" and "Rapt Devotion"
Kitchen Poet: "The Loss of Faith"
Licking River Review: "What I Learned from My Handwriting Analysis"
Literary Review: "Getting Out of the Fast Lane"
Lucid Stone: "When the World Falls Around You"
Michigan Poet: "Falling"
Mississippi Crow: "A Way of Dying"
Muse and Stone: "A Little Night Music"
New York Quarterly: "A Great Vat of Silence"
North American Review: "The Poet Chokes Himself Up"
Oracle: "Middle Age"
Oyez Literary Review: "Another Secret"
Oyez Literary Review and *Poetry in Michigan/Michigan in Poetry:* "My 53rd Autumn in Michigan"
Parting Gifts: "The Curse"
Passages North: "Think Death"
Poet Lore: "Poetry Slam"
Poetry East: "In a Small Town" and "Lost"
Poetry Northwest: "A Process of Aging"
Poetryrepairs: "Flood of Centuries"
Quercus Review: "What If I Don't?"
Rattle: "Lessons"
Raving Dove: "Jackpot of Love"
Red Ochre Literary: "Not Beauty"
Sierra Madre Review: "The World Drinks"
Slant: "Alone No More"
Southern Indiana Review: "Against the Abstract"
Sub-Lit: "Party Animal"
Thundersandwich: "The Leadville Cemetery"
Trebeca Poetry Review: "The Fall and Rise"
Willow Springs: "The Days After"

My gratitude is sent out to all of the great students, teachers, friends, and family who have supported and challenged me through the years, with special thanks to the loving muse of my life, Debra Marie.

Contents

Part I: Listen

What I Learned About My Handwriting Analysis	3
Do Not Give Dogs What is Holy	5
Jackpot of Love	6
Spring and the Theory of Regret	7
Proselytizing	8
The World Drinks	10
Another Secret	11
The Pregnant Woman	13
When the World Falls Around You	14
The Pleasure	16
The Loss of Faith	17
Alone No More	18
Strange Flower	20
Nothing More Sacred Than This	21
Time and History	22
My Savior	24
The Days After	25
In a Small Town	27
Getting Out of the Fast Lane	28
Coming to Terms with the End of the World	29
Why are Shoes Thrown at Newly Married Couples?	30
The God in My Ear	32
Party Animal	33
Falling in Love	34
Not Beauty	36
Lost	38
What I Call Myself	39
The Curse	41
Love is Skin Deep	42
A Great Vat of Silence	43
Rapt Devotion	44
Lessons	45
In the Face of Whatever	46
What Love Is	47

PART II: Dance

The World's a Stage. Not.	51
What Comes to Mind at the End	52
His 53rd Autumn in Michigan	53
Against the Abstract	54
A Way of Dying	55
Falling	56
The Process of Aging	57
A Shedding of the Skin	59
God Lost in the Bread Section	60
The Poet Chokes Himself Up	61
November's Down	63
Middle Age	64
Flood of Centuries	65
What If I Don't?	66
Think Death	67
The Leadville Cemetery	69
The Death in Your Face Game	71
Poetry Slam	72
The Fall and Rise	74
Something Cryptic	75
My Ying and Yang	76
Like Rosencrantz and Guildenstern	77
Dear Past	78
Getting There	79
One Day Like Any Other	81
Thirty More Winters	82
And I Pay for It	83
Last Stand	85
The One After This	86
Borrowed Shoes	87
What I'll Do for You	88
Final Words #1	90
On Your Terms	91
Do the Math	93
A Little Night Music	94

Part I:

Listen

What I Learned About My Handwriting Analysis

I'm asked to write this sentence three times:
>*Everything I am and know can be told
in these few shaky words.*

Right off the bat,
the large issues come to light—
my ease with the unknown,
a preference for folly,
a definitive reliance upon
religion and philosophy.

The missing 'n' in Everything
points clearly to a lack
of breastfeeding as an infant.
The 'y' and 'g' dip below the line
but never come back to right themselves.
Researchers claim this is a clear sign that
I have internal emotional festering:
the desire within to complete
versus the desire to let go.

They list off my siblings,
my early childhood successes,
the secret fort in Lexington Heights.
Because I use both cursive and printing mixed,
they inform me of a latent aggressive tendency
toward society and form in general,
which explains my anti-social patterns,
which inhibits speech, which leads
to my comfort in solitary settings.

By examining only my vowels,
they predict, with 96.2% accuracy,
that I will complete my doctorate.
I will live to see grandchildren.
I will rise above my damaged knees.
I will own a sporty convertible.

And in the final analysis,
as signified by the way I dot my 'i' and end
each sentence with a period,
I will make my peace with the world
in April or May, on a warm and sunny day
when everything will go right for me
except
one thing.

Do Not Give Dogs What is Holy

And do not feed pigs the bacon fat.
Do not place a pillow over the sleeping
woman's mouth, no matter how tempting
that may be.
Do not buy a genuine fur coat for $10
on the corner of Gratiot and Six Mile
from a man with one shoe.
Keep your nose out of other people's affairs
and private parts.
Forget the impossible notion
that the girl on the bus loves you
and wants to have your babies.
Do not let your penis dictate your every move.
Do not swing the tequila bottle
over the head of an asshole,
unless there's no way out.
Never bet on Lucky Legs at the track,
never stick a live wire in your mouth,
never teach your grandmother how to suck eggs.
It should be obvious, in most cases,
what you should do,
and what you should not do.
For God's sake, use your brain a little:
you never carry hot coals in your hands,
never drink a case of Labatt's in one sitting,
never play the piano with a sledge hammer.
Above all, do not give dogs what is holy.
This is the ultimate *faux pas*,
the straw that'll break the collie's back,
the one and only sin that'll send you barking
up the wrong tree for a lifetime,
despising every wag you meet
in this dog-eat-dog world.

Jackpot of Love

"I want to get drunker than I was last April…"
-Charles Boyle

but this time, run through main street singing
like one of the thousands not even considered
for *American Idol*. I want to show the world
I can pick myself up,
try to stay sober and ignore the loud ringing
in my head. I'll find a healthy cowgirl
and make her mine, carry her up to the golden gates
and get a blessing from God herself. I want to see
how life feels when there's love in every crevice
of my day. Let's grab the jackpot—rubies, diamonds, pearls—
and make a home where fantasy
can live like a kind, gentle servant.
I want your face in the corner of every dream,
your words sitting on the tip of my tongue.
When we sleep, I want your hair like seaweed wrapped
around me.
Coursing through my limbs, in my bloodstream,
I want chunks of love clogging my arteries,
knocking me down on my calloused knees. I pray for the strength
to drink your lips, your breath, your dark eyes, your hands,
and fall headfirst into your soul, innocent, for once, washed
clean.

Spring and the Theory of Regret

You can see spring in the storm clouds,
growing on the bare branches,
spring in the yellow tulips out back.
You can hear it in the loud
calling of cardinals,

in the children's voices like an avalanche
of yelling. Everything's alive
with possibility.
Around the new bird house, a goldfinch
does an inventory of risk

like a scholar in some long lost archive.
It's cliché, but the world's born
again and even you can feel it.
Some gear inside
switches on, turning whistles and bells,

churning up feelings you'd sworn
were dead. When that strange woman
stares at you and smiles,
your heart aches, a thorn
cutting through everything you've missed.

PROSELYTIZING

Found written on a bathroom wall—
Jesus Saves.
John 4:16
Jim 11:18
Fred 3:45

Why is it
in every men's bathroom
from the New York thru-way
to elementary schools in Pasadena
God's message is scribbled
on the wall?
Is there some connection between
this basic human act
and the timeliness of the word of God?
Is there a secret connotation
behind calling it a 'john'?

Maybe it has to do with the release of a burden
and a fresh new start, the baptism
of spiritual awakening in the splash of water,
hidden away from the secular world
for a few brief moments...
Maybe there's some obscure allusion
to Noah and the great flood,
to parting of the Red Sea,
manna from heaven after the exodus,
or Jesus' forty nights alone, in meditation,
in Gethsemane.

Outside Syracuse,
after I add my name to the list,
Dave 9:37,
I wipe myself clean,
O God,
saved again.

The World Drinks

Spring is here
crazier than ever.
The morning, sunshine, 60,
turned to dark clouds
& snow flurries,
& by evening, a rainbow,
a bleeding sun over the trees.
Spring, with everything
on her face,
blows into town on a white horse,
hair up in a bandana,
a flask in every pocket.
When she drinks,
the whole world drinks.
Worms go berserk,
in & out of their rainy holes;
robins barely flying,
fatter than cats.
We get used to testing the air
before going out:
spring coat, winter coat, no coat.
But spring is here for good,
lying on the grass,
passed out in the trees,
wading through rivers
in her bare feet.
Before May,
we'll be lifting our mouths to the sky
& drinking whatever she pours on us,
in love, insane,
unsteady in our bodies,
every dream
a wet one.

Another Secret

At every wedding reception
Since high school
I've signed the guest book
I've signed my name
Written in one of my many addresses
And then I've signed Frank Zappa's
Name
Made up an address like
123 Moon Unit Lane
Dweezil California
I've signed Frank Zappa
Into dozens of weddings
My friends my relatives
My wife's friends
And there's no explaining
Why
Zappa's dead and gone
And has been for awhile
But I can't get the thought
Of Frank Zappa
Out of my mind
He's like an uncle or brother or cousin
Taking cuts in the food line
For more corn and cheesy potatoes
Like someone shaking his booty
Out on the dance floor
To 'Proud Mary"
A plain old guy who simply wants
What we want
And who keeps coming back

From the dead
To toast
The newlyweds
Love Frank or
Love Frank Zappa or
Love Franky Z
Writing in the margins
You kids will be just fine
      Trust me

THE PREGNANT WOMAN

she lies on her back
her belly
drooping out
round & tight
& I want to kiss it
& grab it &
lift her up
in the air
over my head
with her warm belly
in my hands
a huge pale cantaloupe
a smooth inner moon
rising & pulling at her
waves of skin
a belly full of dirt & light
water & air
blood & sky
a belly kicking & rolling
& sometimes I just want
to climb inside her
& say *Listen, man,*
you'll never believe
what's out there

When the World Falls Around You

you pick the pieces up
one by one
or in handfuls
& curse under your breath
as you get to the job—
cutting   hammering   gluing
one part to another
until you have the world
back in all its shiny, fleshy
glory

you are on your own here
& everywhere
in the wide fields of new snow
in the cold pines behind
the collapsing barn
on the deer path leading to the salt lick
& for a moment you realize
either the world is at your fingertips
or your fingertips reach to the end of a
world

tomorrow or the next day or next week
a hawk will sail over the treeline
& glide along your eye-way
you'll feel your skin falling off
your bones again
this time you'll know what to do—
take a deep breath
swear into the sky

roll your sleeves back & start
picking the world up
by its tail   its ear   by its short hairs
until it squeals for you & only
you

The Pleasure

"Collin, who likes touching his nipple hair..."
                            -Yasuko

what we do in the privacy of our homes
is sacred, sort of, or should be.

some like to eat grass clippings or take pleasure
pulling off scabs; others worship the foam

in a bubble bath or get off on the agony
of their relatives. there's a section in the brain

that thrives on repetition. we find a zone
in the abyss, and it lights up like a marquee

against the gray matter, etching on the membrane
a peculiar memory for life. as he pulls the hair

out on each nipple, twisting it slightly in his fingers, he sails
above the trees and clouds, into the palaces of the mundane.

THE LOSS OF FAITH
after "Crazy Stuck in Pink" by Leslie Smith

He smokes the King James Bible,
rips out pages from Exodus,
which seems appropriate to him.
Everyone dies, either willing and able
or panicked and in pain.
We're all down here for the famous
trip until God calls out our names
and we plead for more time.
With each cough, there is a cuss
and then another page is torn.
It's his book, dammit, and he aims
to smoke through the Old Testament
by this November or Christmas.
By the look of the flame
in his life, he knows exactly where this will end.

Alone No More
(title of a new German CD)

There's a CD now available,
for those loners by accident, full of sounds
that give the illusion someone else
is with you in the empty apartment or house.
There's a recording of someone coming
through the back door, putting away groceries
(slamming cupboards, stocking cans, opening the refrigerator);
a track of a person lighting a cigarette,
smoking and reading a paper;
a recording of hands washing dishes;
someone vacuuming.
The idea of the CD gets me wondering
about the quirky noises
I take for granted—
the dishwasher cycling,
dog lapping water from his dish,
a telephone conversation, someone whistling,
my son's music droning upstairs,
our parakeet stringing together his litany
of chirps and tweets, a piano playing,
lawnmowers outside on the golf course,
a baby hawk calling for mom,
the toilet flushing,
a huge sigh.
And then I can imagine some lonely young woman
settling down for the night, turning on
the last track titled "Breath,"
a recording of someone breathing,
in and out, over and over,

slow and deliberate,
                as if to say,
You're alive, don't worry, you're alive.

Strange Flower

*"Bees can remember human faces, but only if they are
tricked into thinking that we are strange flowers."*
             "Findings," Harper's, *2010*

Your face, as I've said from day one, blossoms
like a rose, smooth and pink, but it's no trick—
you grow more beautiful with each season,
that flower scent in your hair, on your bare shoulders,
my soul drawn to your brown eyes, your red lipstick.

Like the bees, there's only one good reason
to hover in your arms: to live. I want to be
the stem in your vase, the honey in your hive. I want
to memorize your face and drink your breath until I'm flying,
punch drunk, your love smeared from my head to my feet.

Nothing More Sacred Than This

Let me hold this great day
over my head, chanting
some ancient mantra or prayer,
and dance like a silly clown
painted by a drunken Monet.

Let me see beyond my ignorance,
smell the childhood in your hair.
Let me strip naked and wear the gown
of the future, predicting joy, granting
wishes and desires with eloquence,

lifting the poor out of their holes,
handing over to the meek their crowns.
Above the crying and ranting,
there are no obvious answers:
each of us lives like a troll

in the shadows of his own making.
We rise up to fight, swinging, panting,
doing what we must to protect our lair.
But we learn too late that to breathe is to drown,
and to love is to live with our hearts breaking.

Time and History

*"You could have been just another maggot
squirming over history's roadkill."*
                          -Charles Simic

Whether we invent
a cure for cancer,
break the world record
for a marathon,
or finally get promoted
after working late every night,
adding up the overtime,
neglecting our kids and wives,
we eventually roll over
and become common roadkill:
a squirrel, raccoon, the neighborhood cat.
That doe off the side of the road,
her twisted legs shooting out
in every direction,
says more
about the truth of our existence
than we care to believe.
After the hit,
the flies show up in a matter of seconds.
The crows take a few hours.
By morning, the maggots are munching
their way to new life.
Even in death,
we are useful.
And history, in her beautiful classic car,
speeds ahead of us

like a drunk driver
swerving back and forth,
crashing, hitting, refusing
to slow down or stop
for anyone.

My Savior

> *"And then it is my*
> *own hand in my mouth—I am biting the hand—*
> *cooling me down."*
> -Dennis Hinrichsen

I bite the hand that feeds me, the hand that rises
                toward heaven & blames the stars for everything
wrong. Of course, this after swallowing the last mouthful of
hope left on the table.   I'm tired of the disguise.
I'm lost behind the mask, the intricate but crumbling creed

I have grown to believe.   My only chance is to tie a string
            to you & let you pull me along.
I want your lips burned into my flesh.
                  I want your clean teeth to sink
into my frightened heart, love, until I give in & bleed.

The Days After

1.
After you left
I stared out the window
for three days.

I saw your face blooming
in the fog, dissolving,
sinking down into grass.

I heard your footsteps,
your bare feet indent the carpeting
as if you were walking

through the house,
your quiet voice
blowing words on the back of my neck.

2.
On the fourth night without sleep
the moon was a white tongue
laughing across the sky.
So I rummaged through the house
putting a match
to all the plants you left behind,
throwing out your books, rugs, blankets,
the one painting in the bedroom, your slippers,
your turquoise bracelet.

3.
And that night
when I closed my eyes,
hundreds of bees
caught inside me

started stinging their way out.

In a Small Town

The air is wet and thick
with rain yet to come.
You feel it. You see
the dark clouds lumbering
up from the south,
dragging their clean feet
on the tops of the tallest trees.
One trip and it'll be a downpour,
sending the robins
into the maples to jockey
for position.

Maybe you are right
to sit here alone under the apple tree
watching the traffic of birds,
wind in the leaves,
seven green tomatoes clinging
on for dear life.
Maybe you deserve this.
You could be weeding the garden
or trimming the bushes; you could be
washing the car, sweeping the sidewalk;
you could be folding clothes:

instead, you kill another ant
and stare at the flowers
like some harmless small town god—
yellows, reds, purples—ignorant
of their proper names
but loving them
nonetheless.

Getting Out of the Fast Lane

Explain this crazy life
to me in one sentence
and I'll eat my hat.
I'll eat a book about hats,
spine and all.
So here we are, set down
on this planet, bumped
off of center stage early,
tossed into the wings
without wings, dumped
into the cold, deep end
where we flail to keep
our heads above water.
We sell ourselves
to the lowest bidder
day after day.
There are moments
when all we can do
is fall to our knees
praying for a sign
to end the end of silence.
Let's you and I
leave the world behind—
the kids, jobs, pressure—
and find a quiet place
to settle in.
I want your face to tell me
what the heart demands.
I'll pay up. For you,
I'll carry the moon
into hiding
and shine myself
if I have to.

Coming to Terms with the End of the World

The world walks over me like a doormat,
stomping the dirt off its messy shoes,
taking my talents for granted.

It's to be expected. There are too many of us gnats
buzzing around down here
to focus on only one man or woman, one Muslim or Jew

or Buddhist, one person's dreams of fame.
My truth is not your truth, and their truth
carries no more weight than a decent tattoo.

The questions are universal, but the answers
we take to the grave. There is no shame
in uncertainty, no despair in the unknown.

I'll cheer you on down the road
as you raise a glass in my name,
asking for every tear

to be wiped dry. Each life is blown
through a field of days
with no rhyme or reason.

Close your eyes and call it home:
it's the one and only living cure.

Why are Shoes Thrown at Newly Married Couples?

Some say the tradition
carries over
from an ancient Biblical practice
signifying the transfer of goods, the taking
of something, as in the Psalms—
"Over Edom will I cast out my shoe."
Others believe it stems
from an old custom where the father
presents his daughter's shoe to the groom,
who touches her on the head with it,
claiming ownership.
There's also the belief
that throwing shoes is a reminder
of the past when a woman
was taken by brute force
as her family fought to keep her.
In Turkey, even today,
the bridegroom alone runs
from his guests who fling
slippers at him.

But I like to think of shoe-throwing
as a sign of hope
that the new couple will walk
in each other's soles
and be able to last through
the long journey.
The shoes thrown remind us

of the prints we make,
given time,
through the thick, red forest
of one another's
heart.

The God in My Ear

says Don't
and It'll be okay.
says You should have
  known better.
says I told you so.
says Just wait—
  I've seen what you
  can do.

The voice is
mine
and God's.
I can hear it
in my sleep
and when I drive
to work.
I can hear it
breathing, not saying
a word.

The voice
says Here's an idea:
  why don't you write
  this?
says You deserve
  better.
says Why don't you
  listen to me?
says Why do
  I love you
  so much?

Party Animal

I said you look Asian
to the woman in a red dress
who did not look Asian at all.
I wanted to stand out
from the rest
and be noticed. She said to call
her at 6:32 a.m. or don't bother again.
She downed her girly drink, collapsed
into a briefcase and walked out
under some toad's arm. This is when
I knew the drugs were working. I mapped
out our life together, second by second,
and detailed the next 50 years of bliss
on the side of a toothpick.
Just as I finished, the Mafia gunned
down the bartender and two patrons, but missed
me except for my leg, arm, and lower back.
The blood flowed like milk and honey
and I got so hungry I ate the bar rags,
beer glasses, ashtrays, even hacked
down the dead bartender's keys.
I then flew to Vegas with a flock of robins
who had names like Winifred, Gilbert, Landow,
and we gambled away the last of our pennies
until morning when truth became more like sin.

Falling in Love
for Debbie, my E.R. nurse

1.
She staggers into the emergency room,
bent over,
hair frazzled and dirty,
an old looking young woman
in her twenties.
She's a little overweight,
a little dumpy.

Her medical problem: a hot dog
lost in her vagina.
She's escorted back to the pelvic room
where she undresses,
climbs up into the stirrup chair,
legs spread wide open.
Gloved, the doctor lubricates
the area and reaches in,
groping, searching,
until he finds it.
A Koegel frank, wet and drippy.

2.
At the nurses' station,
everyone's talking.
"That's what I call
getting a piece of meat."
"I've heard of pouring
the pork before,
but this is ridiculous."

"Hell, I bet that dog's
well done by now."
But in the corner
of your mind, you wonder,

How lonely does a woman have to be
to love a hot dog?
At what stage of life
         exactly
      does meat look physically appealing,
      start whispering your name,
      and promise to be all yours?

Not Beauty

"It's not the job of beauty to save us."
                    -Mary Jo Firth Gillett

No, that bitch just stands around in her house of mirrors
Admiring her own legs, hair, figure, dress,
Even the one minor blemish, a mole,
Gleaming like alexandrite on her cheek.
She's for looks only, apparently meant to inspire,
Challenge, create a sense of longing in us peons:
If only we were beautiful . . .
If only we were perfect . . .

I have no interest in beauty if she can't get her hands wet,
Pick up a 2 X 4, recycle the orange rinds, be useful.
We need more than good looks down here
In the real world to survive. We need jobs.
We need dinner. We need to fix the leaking faucet.
We've got to paint the ceiling and stairwell,
Put up the floor moldings.
Beauty won't help us pay the mortgage
Or file this year's tax forms.
"That's not my job," she says. "But *look* at me."

You can have the bitch for all I care.
Once, when I was young and stupid, like everyone,
I thought beauty was the end-all, be-all.
I had to learn the hard way. I had to cut lawns,
Wash dishes, cook, replace the water pump.
I had to change diapers, clean up vomit, swallow aspirins,
Scrub the kitchen floor, do the laundry, shovel the drive.

If beauty won't save us, then give me someone
Hard-working, dependable, with just enough imagination
To pull her own weight, help carry the load,
Be there with a kind word
When this damn world piles up on me
And there's only one way
Out.

Lost

It was a Lutheran camp in northern Michigan. With teepees! Five boys slept inside on cots and at eleven years old, I couldn't imagine a greater adventure. One full week living in a teepee, along with canoeing, hiking trails through the woods, sitting around campfires. At this camp, in 1966, I felt the first needling spark of love or lust as we joined the girls at the lake for swimming.

I don't remember the boy in the picture. Red hair, ribs protruding, long slender legs, an athlete. My body swallowed him decades ago. His knees were flexible; mine crunch. His chest was smooth and flat while my chest is scarred with years and sun and gray hair. His face said, I'm ready for life—bring it on. My face says, I've seen the days open like miracles.

As I hold the picture in my hand, I can't believe this boy is me. In September, my first grandchild will be born, God willing. I'll hold him in my arms, sing him a song, and kiss his soft forehead as he falls asleep. If that skinny boy in front of the teepee was here now, he'd shrug his shoulders and run off into the dark woods.

What I Call Myself
after Monique van den Berg

When I'm down and out
And feel like God is swinging me around
By the short hairs,
I refer to myself in the third person
As Mr. Happy.
When asked if I want fries with my burger,
I say, "Why, yes, Mr. Happy would like fries,
Even though his cholesterol
Is sailing through the roof."
People are stunned at first,
Unsure of my condition,
But soon play along.
"Does Mr. Happy
want paper or plastic?"
"More coffee, Mr. Happy?"
"Is Mr. Happy sad today?
Tell me about your relationship
With your mother…"

After a few days
Of Mr. Happy, I'm able to feel
The sunshine again, sleep
Without dreaming of train accidents,
Carry on a casual conversation
Without weeping.
I put Mr. Happy on a shelf in the closet,
Within reach, next to the box of winter hats.
I picture him smiling away
In the dark,

Enjoying the solitude of coats,
Time to reflect.
I imagine he thinks up ways
To kill me.

The Curse

"The grandeur of man lies in that he knows himself to be miserable. A tree does not know that it is miserable."
                              -Blaise Pascal

1.
The hawk
glides high above the goldenrod,
turning on a sleeve of wind.
In the light rain, tulips dance and shake,
the yellows becoming neon,
the red, lips.
Stepping into a stream,
a fawn bends to drink,
lifting her head at the call of a dove.
The willow's hair sweeps
the grass, dripping with late spring,
brushing the earth clean.

2.
Tired and unshaven,
slumped in a Lazy Boy,
the man eats a slice of cheese
and washes it down
with a bottle of cheap gin.
There's a loaded gun
on the table.
And each thought
that comes to him tonight
is proof
of his greatness.

Love is Skin Deep

He stands by the hotel window, his limp penis touching the cold glass. In the other room, he hears the hot water rushing in the bathtub. He turns away and stretches. A young child runs down the hallway, screaming outside his door. He can't tell whether it's a sad scream or a happy scream.

Suddenly, he remembers Lydia's face, and how it contorted and scrunched up like a red ball of worms when she said she needed "her space." He was suffocating her, she said.

Without thinking, he leaves the room, one couple outside gasping at his nakedness. If only my body would open and puke out the past, he thinks, I could live with it. He reaches the door to the parking lot, exits, lays down in the snow, and makes an angel. He stands, his skin blotched red from the cold. "Here's to Lydia," he says and pees in the angel's face.

A Great Vat of Silence

It's one of those days
in a life of a lot of those kind of days
when you want nothing more than to curl up and sleep,
bury yourself in a blaze
of dreams and sink down

toward the core of time, so deep
it hurts to wake up. You drown
inside your own darkness.
You lie still, floating, deaf to the world's sounds:
the wind chime on the tree, the children yelling

across the street. It's a day when it seems best
to chuck it all,
throw in the towel, toss out the baby
with the bath water, to leap out of the moment and fall
into that great vat of silence.

But you don't. You pull yourself up, look around, a refugee
stunned by the sunlight arcing through the window.
You walk outside and breathe in the autumn air,
cool and decaying, stare at the willow
dancing in the wind and, for now, go on.

Rapt Devotion

When her husband fell asleep, the wife would secretly wrap him in gift paper. Or parts of him—hands and arms, each toe neatly done, sometimes his whole head and other times just an ear or lock of hair. Two or three times per year, she'd gift wrap his penis in metallic gold paper.

For an insomniac, she was productive in her own way. Her reasoning went like this: each day was a miracle, and her husband was a gift, so he should be properly presented to the world. She'd spend thirty or forty minutes carefully folding an intricate corner for his big toe. It was a labor of love. And before sunrise and his stirring toward light, she unwrapped each part of him quietly, slowly, so as not to hinder one minute of sleep.

As her husband awoke, the wife lay down and closed her eyes, pretending to rouse from a deep sleep. The husband swung his legs off the bed, stood and stretched high into the air.

"You look like a gift from God," she said.

"I feel like one," the husband replied.

"Good," said the wife, smiling.

Lessons

"Is there anyone among you who, if your child asks for a fish, will give a snake instead of a fish? Or if the child asks for an egg, will give a scorpion?"
                    Gospel of Luke, Chapter 11

She asks for pop, I pour cold water.
He asks for Kool-Aid, I pour cold water.
She asks for toys, I buy gum.
He asks for the hammer, I tell him to look for it.
Asks for chocolate, I peel an orange.
Asks for money, I dish out chores.
They ask for help, I give them help.
She asks for ice cream, I fix lunch.
He asks for a sip of beer, I pour cold water.
Asks for understanding, I offer advice.
Asks for more time, I give excuses.
They ask for a later curfew, I say no.
She asks for a swimming pool, I take her to the beach.
He asks for it big time, I give it to him big time.
They ask and ask, I give and give.
So when they finally ask for answers,
I give them love.
They ask for their freedom,
I give them love.
And when they ask for love,
I give them
everything.

In the Face of Whatever

In the sunlight, you glow, a carp
ready to hunker down and lie on the bottom
of anything for a while. Your big fish eyes

look up at me, glassy and dark, shining.
I'm hooked. Again. You throw your damn voice
in my direction and I gladly take the bait.

There's no defense against love, or something
close to it. My body tingles, hundreds of minnows
streaking up and down my legs. My eyes glaze over
and all the way through until the sunlight pours

down on you, washing that brown skin in waves,
picking the curves out of your body and framing them
for me, placing the best parts of you
in full view, in crystal clear view. I want your lips
on every inch, your hair on every piece of furniture,

your breath melting into the bare skin
on my neck and chest. Let's wade here, alone,
in a pool of love, wet and anxious to make it
last a lifetime or two, to splash and laugh

in the face of whatever's out there or up there
or down there. I want your bones touching
my bones, your spinal cord fused to my cord,

your face permanently mounted on the wall
of my eyes so I can see you when I swim
down into my dreams at night and drown.

What is Love

*"Yeah, right, this is what every girl dreams of—
to be compared to a carp."*
                                  -Debra James

My love poem likening you to a carp
was purely metaphorical.
A carp is really a beautiful creature,
with bold, strong fins,
sturdy build, adaptive,
a survivor if there ever was one.
The poem was not meant to denigrate,
nor to be a sucker-lip comparison
or bottom-feeder analogy by any stretch.
I was thinking about the graceful
speed and turns, those rare jumps
out of water, the ability to see through
the murky depths around you,
the boldness to writhe at the surface
and fight for what you want,
what you deserve.

Any poet worth his salt can compare women
to roses or birch trees or gazelles,
stars or clouds or angels,
but to take a carp as the instrument of my love,
to use the mundane and base
and raise it up to swim in that sacred space
we fill for each other
is far more romantic.
If that carp isn't like your heart
skimming under the dock of my heart,
then frankly
I don't know what love is.

PART II:

Dance

The World's a Stage. Not.

This is not a play. There are no lines
to rehearse, no lights

to step into, no rise and fall
of a curtain, no spine

of a plot to map out.
There is no director in sight;

no stage manager to blame
for the missing prop, a broken lamp.

Here and now, you write
your lines as they happen,

waiving any notion of fame.
Though there is no stage

you walk out hoping for applause,
expecting to see your name

in bright letters across the marquee,
but the sign's blank. No page

to turn, no blocking to remember.
Each day you wake to play a part

full of sorrow and kindness, laughter and rage,
and it's all for an audience of one.

What Comes to Mind at the End

February, a cold morning, Friday,
and we bury another friend.
We're at that age, you know,
when people begin to say goodbye
to this earth, and find their way

back to mere dust. There's a long
path that weaves through the snow,
descending below a gray sky.
We all walk it in the end.
Our lives light up like a song

and then flash into nothing.
Silence becomes a stifled cry,
and time lifts its bandage to mend
the wound. But when it's our turn to go,
there won't be angels on wings

or chariots blazing from above:
we'll simply lean over or fall or bend
down and die. The north wind will blow,
relatives and friends will come, then drive
home, worrying about the end of love.

His 53rd Autumn in Michigan

Early November and it comes down to this again: the man sheds, losing his hair, ears, face, a leg dropping in the driveway, his arms torn loose, blown across the yard like fleshy styrofoam. He dissolves into an autumn day, his soul turning that pale shade of sky gray. It happens every year as the evening temps flirt with 30, as trees strip down to scarred bark, as certain birds become memories.

He resigns himself to this fact of living, which is like a fire, bright and consuming at the same time. Thick, cut logs are tossed into the flames; within hours, they're glowing piles of ash, sparking up in the stiff wind.

The man waits for spring when he hopes to reassemble for another year, to piece himself together with what's left from the bitter winter months. This ear is not working well; that arm carries a peculiar ache; his left eye trembles now. As with every blessing, there's a price to pay.

Against the Abstract

"An abstract object, invisible or non-existent, does not belong to the domain of art . . . show me an angel, and I'll paint one."
                                         -Gustave Courbet

Forget love. Hate. Fear.
Forget the spirit.
No more longing, justice, hope.
Disregard anything you can't hold,
Smell, or see. Our lives winnow down
To the bare elements, the obvious,
The mundane. There is no soul.
There is no heaven.
There is no God.
There is no lust: only flesh
And sweat and movement.
There is no forgiveness:
Simply a man crying, burying his face
In his hands, trying to place words
Into the dry air.
Forget pleasure, joy, courage.
If it has no color, no form, ignore it.
Focus on hands, eyes. On skin,
Leaves, apples, laughter, moon, trees.
One crow circles
Above the field, dusk approaching,
But it's not loneliness, not despair,
     Not desire.
No matter what we may want to believe:
It's a black crow gliding on air,
Looking for something dead
To eat.

A Way of Dying
for Leonard Nolens

  When he writes, particularly a poem, he ends up dying. It's always unexpected. The final question mark on the page rips loose and strangles him on the living room floor. Or the pen turns slowly toward him and then rams straight through his heart. Sometimes the ink smell, rising up into the air, poisons him.
  The end of each poem is a birth and a death, and the writer has no choice but to die over and over in bizarre ways—bludgeoned by a period, overdosed by a word entering his bloodstream, knifed by an idea.
  One day, that last poem will be standing out in the rain, watching as others lower the writer into the ground. After the family leaves, the poem will walk over, throw a handful of dirt on the coffin, and wander off, looking for a home.

Falling

I've wheelbarrowed over a thousand
apples behind the cedars
for compost.
Hundreds are still left stranded
in the branches, dropping with each burst
of wind. Every year's a blur,
and my heart marks another tally off
inside my chest wall. This is the year
of my first grandson, who purrs
asleep in my arms, who looks through me
with his dark eyes. I touch his soft
cheeks and his little fists shoot out
as if to catch himself.
We're all falling into the great trough,
I want to say, but don't.

I can't imagine his world without
imagining the end of mine.
Who will sit in this lovely yard
and write poems? There's no doubt
someone will, someone from this dying planet
who will look over at the pines
and remember his past and smile.
The wind will blow apples
down, the autumn sun will shine,
and he'll hear the jay calling
for no reason other than to file
a complaint that the bird bath
is dry as a bone.
In the end, we all bow our heads in exile,
and prepare, in our own ways, for the fall.

The Process of Aging

The world falls apart
by the simple touch
of my hand—
my sons shrink,
fade back against
the wallpaper.
The closer I get
the smaller they become,
a tack, a needle head,
a grain of salt.

My daughter, however, floats,
bobbing up at the ceiling,
holding her hands over her ears
as I plead with her.
When the door opens,
she sails out,
a pale, human balloon,
waving to everyone
but me.

With a firm hug,
my wife collapses into dust,
ruining my shirt and pants.
After this many years together,
I've learned to brush her aside
and get on with things.

But my powers are growing.
Now a mere stare will melt

the dog, take leaves off
of bushes, stun the politician
with complete silence.
I simply think about touching
my father and he dies;
innocent dreams
demolish buildings,
lay whole forests to waste.

I stumble down the street,
sidewalk exploding behind me,
trees cracking, cars losing
doors and tires and side panels.
The day breaks open
across the sky, stretching,
coming apart, it seems,
at every joint.
The moment I think
it will never last,
it won't.

A Shedding of the Skin
for Herb Scott

A man's body stops,
       silent and still, and, if lucky,
              he leaves behind memories
flashing in the minds of a few,
                    words lodged on the tongues
              of those who knew him well.
His legacy,   like a highway billboard,
      rises briefly along the horizon
           and is gone.

       Life is a bird nesting in the apple tree out back;
             it's a stopped up drain;
it's a half moon easing behind
                      the dark clouds.
Life flies around and offers a gift box
        to some, a pail of needles to others.
     Offers to a few a cold drink of water;
to others,   a plateful of mud.

The world of *what if* gets caught
       in the throat on a daily basis,
    right next to the universe
               of *if only*.
There's one guarantee down here:
               regret. And there's
one regret:
to not have another chance.

God Lost Somewhere in the Bread Section
a line from Jack Ridl's poem

Something draws him
to the bakery side of stores—
the smell of warm bread, the thought
of dough rising and baking,
more than a hint of melted butter
brushed across the tops
of steaming loaves.

Whatever the reason, it's enough
to make God lose his usual
good sense of direction.
He wanders back and forth
through the bread section, imagining this loaf of rye
with some pastrami and ham;
the sour dough with smoked turkey,
Dijon mustard, a red onion;
the French with melted Gouda and salsa;
a homemade pumpernickel toasted,
smothered in cream cheese.

If one sad day, you're in the store
with your life crumbling around your ankles,
look for an old man wandering
through the bread aisle, lost in dreams,
a face chiseled out by time and memory.
Walk over to him,
close your eyes
and open your mouth:
he'll place bread on your tongue,
forgive you
for taking so long.

THE POET CHOKES HIMSELF UP
after John Rybicki, who choked himself up

every time he writes
he cuts a thin slit down
the middle of his chest, pulls out
the heart, and throws it on
the blank page.
what's left after
cleaning up
is a poem.
by this time in his life
he's learned to keep the deep cut open,
easy access when inspiration
strikes.
but sometimes the heart falls out
into his palms for no reason
and he stuffs it home.
when he makes love to his wife,
the heart often drops onto her chest,
an apt metaphor, and she strokes it
before placing it back
where it belongs.

this is why poets don't live
as long as fiction writers.
the poet's heart,
used and reused for each poem,
tossed and dragged across the page,
bleeds its words into
poems, poems into
tears, tears into blood which

creates more poems.
once you begin,
there is no way to stop
this
bleeding.

November's Down

    A few last leaves
hang on the maples like cancer,
unwilling to let go and fly,
unable to drop to their knees
before falling face first
    at the end of another year.
There are no words of praise
beautiful enough to stop
the winter from landing, to cure
the month of its lonely cold.
    Sometimes you're left to raise
your fists to the dark sky
and pray
for more time, more grace,
for more love than is humanly possible.

MIDDLE AGE

We laughed and danced
during the thunderstorm from hell.
The lightning was a strobe light,
the thunder, an immense
bass line trailing off in the distance.
And then you stopped and said,
"I don't know this one. Let's sit it out."
"You want another whiskey?" I asked.
"Sure," you said, "while we catch our breath."

I ordered two shots at the bar.
We sat on the floor and drank, wishing
we were younger and could go all night
like we used to, wishing we could start
over, dreaming that the rain would
wash us back into children
and we'd cower in our mother's arms
as the storm broke open every fear
in our little worlds.
You started to cry.
"Don't," I said. "It'll pass."
"That's exactly what
I don't want to happen," you said.

Flood of Centuries

"Entomologists working in Iran and Turkey learned that a rare species of solitary bee builds brood chambers of brightly colored flowers."
                              Harper's, *July 2010*

Even bees get depressed,
down in the flower dumps of bee-dom.
Everyone needs
some alone time, space to remind yourself
there's only one chance
to get it right, or semi-right,
or done in a way
that won't embarrass you.
In dreams, the bee discovers
a blossom larger than an oak tree,
waterfalls of pollen
roaring out. In life,
he heads to the brood chamber,
punching his fists through walls,
screaming at the top of his tiny lungs.

I'm no hero. The good parts of me
crumble off my shoes like dried mud.
If I'm lucky, I'll come to terms
living as a footnote
in the flood of centuries.
If not,
I'll need more than a fucking brood chamber
to stay alive.

What If I Don't?

"You must change your life."
                    -Rainer Maria Rilke

The world will limp forward
dragging its bad leg
as before.
Night will arrive on schedule
and paint my windows black.
Autumn will cry out its last breath
as winter, pale and starving,
falls from the sky,
a heap of bleached bones.

If anything, I don't want
my life to change: I want the clocks
to break so Time can sit on my couch,
drink soda and nibble cookies,
lounge in an afternoon sun spot.
We'll talk about our childhood dreams;
we'll laugh at the well of the past.
Watch some old movies.
Prepare a dinner fit for a queen.
Share a slice of peach pie.
And when we put our feet up
and doze a bit, sinking
into a sweet sleep,
nothing will be there
to wake us.

Think Death
for Richard Shelton

I don't think Death
has much in store for us—
maybe a sale on silence,
a discount on all the darkness
we can carry.
Lowering ourselves into the ground,
blocking out any chance of sun or moon light,
what do we expect?
Death is a hoarder by nature.
He keeps grabbing, pulling things
into him—dogs, insects, fish,
rhinos, trees, us.
A dark mass burrowing
under the surface,
his eyes are open,
his hands forever clenched.

The idea that we live
a second life, or third,
makes for good science fiction
but no one really believes it.
We're born, we die.
In and out. Up and down.
Truth and truth.
In death,
the rich and poor,
the cursed and blessed,
all enter through the same door,
wide open from above,
locked tightly from below.

I don't think Death
has much to offer us
other than free cold storage,
a stillness close to infinity.
From birth, throughout our lives,
we create an enormous debt,
owing our parents, brothers, aunts,
neighbors, teachers, sisters.
In death,
even someone who is a credit
to society gets tallied in the loss column.

I don't think Death
wishes us any ill will.
He's got a job to do.
He adds up each life,
totaling each breath, each sin,
and when it's time,
he cashes in on us,
the ringing from his ancient register
like church bells
in the distance.

The Leadville Cemetery

A precious one from us is gone
A voice we loved is stilled
A place is vacant in our home
That never can be filled
    Alice King, 1889
    10 yrs old

The names in the cemetery
break the morning air
as I say them out loud,
words forming like bluejays,
awkward and angry.
  Westella Timberlake, 1947
  Lena Muselman, 1887
  Daniel D. Field, 1906
  Jessie E., 1886
One tombstone marks
the bare essentials:
  Walter Donahue
  July 12, 1887
  3 yrs, 10 mos, 2 day
Some I can't read, people
scraped away after decades
of rain and snow and neglect.
Others are surrounded by ornate
wrought-iron fences, feeble attempts
to keep something out
or something in.

As I wander from grave to grave,
I see the wisdom of being buried
in Leadville, 10,200 feet up,

as close to heaven as possible.
I want my resting place here
in full view of Mt. Elbert and Mt. Massive
so I can watch the mountains spread
across the horizon.
Some geologists claim this range
is still forming, increasing
in height two inches every year.
I like the thought of moving upward
toward the planets and stars,
rising toward light, toward wind,
up into the swaying trees
even after death.
Especially
after death.

The Death in Your Face Game

Start by attending a funeral.

Stare long and hard at the powdered face
in the casket,

but picture your child there, a lover, your father,
imagine your own head on the cushion to replace

the dead, like a rotting melon in a basket.
Remember, and number, all the hours

you've flushed down the drain,
all the friends you've forgotten,

the utter nonsense you've devoured
in the name

of living your own life. That's bullshit.
You know it, they know it, this dead guy

knows it. It's time now to raise
your weeping face into the moonlit

sky, pray for the strength of grace to crucify
the past on the closest tree.

Those who live from this moment on, win.
Those who grind a path toward next week

or next year get blown away like human debris.

POETRY SLAM

I'm reading in an important poetry journal
& I like poetry
but I don't understand any of these poems
& then Billy Collins' voice enters my brain
to say "Fuck it. Don't even try, you lame excuse for a poet"
I didn't know Billy was such an asshole
he always seemed like a nice guy to me
though I've never met him in real life
unless you consider this real life which I do
all these award winning poems & books of poems
& chapbooks of poems & most
I can't make heads or tails of
either I am a lame ass poet which could be true
I am a lame ass husband & brother & friend etc.
or there's a conspiracy
a whole lot of poets in the world are writing shit poems
giving each other grants & tenure & reviews
in the *New Yorker* & prize money & endowed chairs
just to spite me
I know Billy Collins isn't in that group
because I get some of his poems
even if I shouldn't
& it seems like these conspirators own
the university presses & lit magazines
& work for the Guggenheim & Provincetown
& suck down martinis with everyone even remotely
associated with the N.E.A.
so here we are living in a country
where so few people actually read poems
at least for pleasure & I figure it won't be long

before the very last poem will be tacked up on a wall
in some governmental museum framed in soft blue lights
where overweight pre-diabetic middle school kids
falling out of buses on field trips will walk by in single file
& glance up at the ink letters on paper wondering
    whatever happened to all the poets
    where did their beards go
    why did they stop writing
but mostly
    why can't I understand what the hell
that poem means

The Fall and Rise

Our lives fall around our feet, blowing away
in a November wind. The sooner we accept this fact,
the better: the world sheds like loose bark. We drive out
to visit my uncle in a nursing home on Sunday.
Legs swollen, hooked up to an oxygen tank, he can't walk
farther than to his bathroom and back.
Time has him cornered, leaning toward his very own hole.

Our children tumble in every direction:
one in Japan, another Milwaukee, the third packed
and aching to move to North Carolina, ready to grab the bull
by its uneven horns. But this is all old
news: each minute peels away a dream or desire,
each hour spills on the floor, used or not, cherished or not.
We're carried along in the flood of days wearing a blindfold
in the end, regardless of who we are or what we've done.

Stone by stone, act by act, we build an empire
of the mundane, the everyday, and carry our small lives
forward on these shoulders of doom.
When our bodies return to ash, burned in the great fire
or eaten by worms, we'll float up to the heavens. Or not.

Something Cryptic

He feels his bones breaking apart inside his skin.
When he considers what the day will bring,
        he sees nothing but black mud, manure, torn limbs
                and guts, a June bug pinned
to white cardboard, a hole in the damp earth.

So on this sky blue day, the seventeenth day of spring,
    he decides to end it once and for all—
the screams in his ears, the glass in his throat, the slice
carved down the middle of his limp heart. He imagines wings
as an angel, sailing among the clouds,

diving in and out of God's golden waterfall.
He finds paper and writes a note, something cryptic
              like "The end comes in the sun's face."
As he takes out a razor blade, he hears a cardinal's call.
He looks down: tattooed in blue on both wrists, the word
DON'T.

My Ying and Yang

I could say today's the first day
of the rest of my life
or I could say
I'm one minute closer to cremation.
The winter sun shines off
the couple inches of new snow outside
and I wonder when I'll get up the energy
to cross-country ski.
The skis are down from the attic,
the poles stare at me
as I stumble through the garage.
I need to exercise.
I need to lose weight.
I need to work myself and what's left
of the muscles I used to own.
Give me some direction, or willpower,
or guts, or nerves, I pray
to whatever or whoever will listen.
I could be thankful for everything or I could wallow
in the muck of my making.
Look, my kids are growing up and moving out,
my old world crumbles and falls,
my body won't do what I ask it to do,
my bones ache, my ears grow hair
faster than I can cut.
But it's all life, they say, brutal, scenic, invisible, lumbering
along at its own god-damned pace.
I eat, I sleep, I work.
Each minute carves a thin scar down the face of my heart.
This could be what it's like to live,
    or
to slowly die.

Like Rosencrantz and Guildenstern
for Tom Stoppard

You're on a boat to nowhere fast
convinced by the illusion of control.
You sail toward the mainland
where, you believe, the truth will come
to light and the missing become whole.

The answers are waiting to be found,
or misplaced, or rewritten. You lift up the spyglass,
searching for a sign of life on the horizon.
But the future arrives in one of two ways:
either it's fluid and random, or it's cast

in stone, inescapable. It can't be both.
As another sun goes down
in the west, you prepare for the worst:
the world careens out of your hands
as ninety coins, all heads, flip toward the ground.

Dear Past

I wish you would get lost
like one of those trophies
from childhood, packed away
in old newspapers in my mother's attic.
Or I wish you would at least
stay behind me where you belong.
You had your day—
now let it go.

What happened one rainy night
in September 1976, or by the pond
in 1982, or in Bay City, 1993,
may be of interest
from a historical point of view
but it has no relevance for me.
It's over, ka-put, nada, boiled
in that vast void of time.
It's in Neverland with Peter Pan,
sailing happily into my own internal
Bermuda Triangle.

You are dead, my friend,
and dredging you back into today's air
will not make the past any different:
It won't make me wiser or more handsome,
won't bring my hair back or shrink this stomach.
You can't change a damn thing in my life.
I take a step forward
and I hear you whining,
one full step behind me.

Getting There

"we are all terminal cases..."
                    -John Irving

Give me the pale red sky
blooming over the pines,
the morning thick
with melting snow and sparrows.
Give me the sweet face of my wife
to kiss,
my daughter dragging her quilt
downstairs to nestle under my arm.
Each day,
the world rises to the occasion.
In all its glory and pain,
it greets me at the door
and we start off,
both of us knowing
where it's all going to end,
but pretending to care less.
Some say the end justifies
the means;
I say the end means
we have to justify ourselves.
We make this life better
or we make it worse.
It's a long walk
down the side of the mountain,
but God, what a view.
Give me the night glowing
with ten million stars,

the wind stepping up to rattle ice
off the oldest willow in town.

No matter how hard
we want to believe
             otherwise,
we're stuck with truth.

One Day Like Any Other

He was found on the kitchen floor, skin blue
                     as a spring sky, dead & gone for hours.
As friends, what can we say
                                         or do
to ease the pain, fill the loneliness, obscure
the raw guilt of the wife? It's a Monday
                     from hell.
At 54, everyone agrees he was too young.
       "I just want him to wake up," she cries,
shaking   wide-eyed   repeating the phrase like a magic spell
                     that won't take. She'll cry out one lung
tonight, another tomorrow, & then at the funeral service.
    Nothing we say will bring him back.
        Nothing we do will remove the knife from her heart.
The world crumbles at the tips of her fingers, a fine black mist.

Thirty More Winters

In the rain, September climbs into a muddy hole
& pouts. It's the end of summer, blah, blah,
the start of fall. Deal with it.
The seasons click through their steps
faster every year, hunched like trolls
under the bridge, wielding chainsaws,
cutting me down to size.
Thirty falls left, if I'm lucky.
Either way, I'm walking
downhill into the great hurrah,
blindfolded & shrinking, just another disguise
in this play between waking
& dreaming. So it's one more September
under my belt—hypertension, high cholesterol,
acid reflux. Beneath the weight of blue skies,
I watch a tree breaking
into clumps of red & light yellow.
The rain will pound the leaves into the ground,
snow will come, the world here will slowly freeze.
And then spring will arrive, ugly & wet, shaking.

And I Pay for It

These words puke out
of my pen, spraying letters
and lines everywhere.
I have no control.
They say what they want,
go where they need to
without prodding.
I'm the bottle of Jack Daniels,
the 12-pack, the cheap wine.
I'm the toilet bowl.
The words use me up
and toss me aside when they're finished.
I watch the pen cough, grunt, let it all
come loose down the page,
wet, stinking, chunks of life
rising and flowing.
Sure, I'm left to clean up
but I can take no credit for this
or any of the others.
This sickness comes in fits and starts,
more intuition than intention,
more luck than divinity.
The pen wretches before passing out
on the floor, hair disheveled,
stains dripping down the front of its shirt.
Tomorrow, it'll wake up
with a huge headache, nauseous, and wonder
what the hell happened.
The poems will be there,
staring

like women waiting to be paid,
chewing gum,
hiking up their skirts,
wiping ink off their full
and beautiful lips.

Last Stand

I'm at that age I can let it all hang out,
every wart and pimple and scar.
Every one of my stupid and embarrassing mistakes
can go up in bright lights and I don't give a damn.
I'm fed up with hope, beyond doubt,

and I've decided to reward my bad self with a break
from courtesy and civil behavior.
I can smell the end of this ride
and it stinks to high heaven.
I'm gonna howl into the night sky, walk naked through the lake,

laugh in the face of custom, swallow the last of my pride
with a glass of Jack Daniels, a knob job
and a bowl of soup. The end is all mine.
Nothing's gonna stop me smiling
from ear to ear, my eyes so wide

that the greenest pines
will look fluorescent, the rain like polished crystal,
the full moon claimed as my very own star.
Everywhere I look, a new world rises out of the ground.
Each breath goes down like a mighty fine wine.

So you can have your jewels and yachts, your expensive cars;
you can work your balls off like someone cares.
I'm grabbing what's left of this glorious world
as I waltz down the side of the mountain,
filling up my torn dance card.

THE ONE AFTER THIS

In my next life,
I'll French kiss the moon
and carve my name on history's tired face.
Doubt will not exist around me.
Fear will be banished; hesitation
will drown in the Lake of Certainty.
I'll shout and jump.
I'll watch every sunset, every
thunderstorm, every snowfall.
I'll laugh and roll and tumble.
My hands will be like eyes,
my feet, curious wheels;
my brain will dive and turn
like a summer bat in the attic.
I'll look for the silver lining, the half-full
glass, the diamonds in the rough,
rainbows, birds, clouds, music.
When death comes near me,
I'll smile and say thanks,
what took you so long, I'm ready,
let's do this the right way, brother.
My next life will stand up on its own two feet,
push out its chest,
    head high,
and sing
as if everything in the world, living or not,
       had ears.

Borrowed Shoes

*"It's also necessary
to be dying"*
                              -Tadeusz Rozewicz

i forget this, among all the rushing and working, chores
and eating, the dressing, the appointments, the laundry.
i'm at that age when i need to start dying
in earnest. with exercise and meds, i might have thirty more
years to make my presence known—write that epic poem,
travel through ireland, mold myself into a memory
my grandchild will recall with kindness.
it's not fair: after a half-century on solid dirt,
i now have my bearings, i know the territory.
the morning frost calls my name; the sunset feels like home.
just when i get comfortable in my skin, no longer a guest
in borrowed shoes, the end rises in the night sky
like a second moon, a dim spotlight i can't escape.
so i start dancing for no particular reason, slow and grotesque,
            auditioning for a part in the unknown.

What I'll Do for You

I'll put everything I know
under a fingernail so you can
scrape it out like manure.
I'll put my advice on an eyelash
or two: listen to the wind
pounding in the waves,
marry after college,
look beyond the obvious,
always obey your heart.
I'll cough up my appendix for you.
I'll drive to Toronto. I'll make ice and
every decent-sounding vegetarian dish
in the damn book. I'll scramble eggs and
change the oil and return the overdue movies.
Give me your worries—I'll bury them
in the yard. Give me your heartache—
I'll hug you back to health or die trying.
Give me your dreams and I'll catalog them,
provide interpretations, commentary.
Hell, I'll even make a few come true.
I'll stop the night from falling,
if you need me to; I'll carry you safely
over the coals; I'll stand in front of any
train; I'll swim across the ocean.

And when I die, I'll save a cloud for you,
a firm white one. I'll have it dry-cleaned,
pressed, lightly starched.
I'll take care of things from this end.
Live your life—laugh, cry, love, hug.

And when your name is finally called,
I'll be waiting at the pearly gates
with a dozen roses and a smile so big
you'll forget there ever was an
Earth.

Final Words #1

"Either that wallpaper goes, or I do."
                              -Oscar Wilde

On his deathbed,
Oscar is telling jokes,
making people smile right up to his end.
Like a young boy whistling as he steps
down into the dark basement,
Wilde taunts death.
But there is no escape,
no comedic turn of events
that would allow him to jump out of bed,
fully dressed, and become the center
of attention again.
This is an ultimatum he can't win,
which is why his family and friends gather
to pull the blanket up to his chin,
bring him a glass of water or warm tea,
wipe the sweat from his forehead.
      May we all die
in the company of those
who are ready
to rip down that ugly wallpaper
if it would make a difference.

On Your Terms

You died the way you lived,
on your own terms,
dropping heart first to the ground.

You had your reasons
for ignoring every good piece of advice
out of a doctor's mouth,

but you kept them to yourself.
It was too little too little
when it came to your health.

"This is what not to do, son," you'd claim.
Or "Do as I say, not as I do."
We'll miss your full body bear hugs;

we'll miss your annual trap shoot;
your knowledge of brakes and rotors and tractors;
how to safely hook up the gas stove.

On November 14th every year, I'll light a candle
and envision you, giddy as a schoolboy,
unable to calm yourself and sleep:

opening day of deer season as soon as
night melts into the bark of trees.
There are regrets, of course, always

and for everyone, but this isn't the place
for that list of grievances and defeats.

For now, in our imaginations,
you are standing at the pearly gates, clapping your hands,
ready and willing to grab whatever piece
of joy is near,

whatever moment of happiness happens
to walk up to you.
"Let's go," you say, and the world jumps on your back,

laughing into the next round of darkness.

Do the Math

In nineteen years, I'll be seventy.
Now a lot can happen
in that much time,
but I don't want to be
cloistered away with eight cats,

banished to my den,
afraid of the boys in the neighborhood,
wondering if I can afford
my meds and then
buy a few groceries as well.

I don't want to be misunderstood
or forgotten, and I don't need
anyone's pity either.
If I can walk, I'll be good.
If I can bend over to tie

my shoes, and lift the fork to feed
myself, I'll make it all right.
Nineteen years is a lifetime
in some tribes, some creeds.
I can see the end of the tracks,

stopping like a bird in mid-flight.
It's time to sing arias, to stare for hours
as the clouds kiss and mate, to smell the trees,
to get out there into the world as each night
comes along, slowly, sadly, calling out names.

A Little Night Music

"Price a British company charges to have a deceased person's ashes pressed into a package of 30 vinyl records: $4,704."
Harper's, *December 2010*

You have my permission:
                press me into a record, a classic,
  one you'll bring out at parties and reunions, one you'll put on
              late at night, forlorn, when you're standing

on the cliff of one of those month-long depressions.
           Let a part of me soothe you back
                              into life.
            Let the music lift and carry you
from the steep edge to a warm cave, a small fire lighting
                   the walls, a pot of stew
     boiling in the hot coals.
     It's a small price to pay for sanity: $156.80 per album.
              That's less than two hours
            with a decent therapist.

Invest in a good record player. Carefully set the album on,
  lift the needle.
            You can imagine my face
                  as you sing, remember my body
    as you dance alone in the living room.
              Picture me sitting there, tapping my foot,
    watching you move slowly across the floor,
              smiling and happy
                    again.

Available from The Fly Came Near It

Old Northwest Review, Fall 2014
Edited by Brandon James Anderson

Old Northwest Review is a literary journal that specializes in publishing poetry and prose that is of, from, and aligned with the culture and aesthetic of the Great Lakes region and the greater Midwest. The Fall 2014 issue includes interviews with Emmy® Award-winning actor, Jeff Daniels, and award-winning poet, Monika Zobel, as well as work from 12 poets and six writers.

I've Had Bigger and Other Things My Wife Said
by Jeff Rice

Did you ever want to prank your wife everyday, write about the results, and publish them online without her knowledge? That's exactly what Jeff Rice did in 2011. Now, the popular blog series is available as a book for the first time ever, revised and updated with an all-new conclusion from the author. Don't miss how this prank ends.

Thanksgiving with Pop-Pop
by K.M. Zahrt

Tommy Tyler asks his eccentric grandfather, Pop-Pop, to tell stories at the Thanksgiving table. Against the wishes of Tommy's mother and grandmother, Pop-Pop dishes out four tales not suitable for a young boy nor reverent for Thanksgiving conversation. He tells of the town's people acting greedily and jealously, committing crimes and adultery, and attempting suicide.

For more information about The Fly Came Near It, visit **MichigandersPost.com**.

Made in the USA
Middletown, DE
24 June 2015

WATERFORD TWP. PUBLIC LIBRARY
5168 Civic Center Drive
Waterford, MI 48329